Bugs

Lucy Bowman

Designed by Josephine Thompson

Illustrated by Ruth Rivers

Bugs consultant: Dr. Margaret Rostron

Reading consultant: Alison Kelly, Roehampton University

Contents

Little and large

Bugs are insects, spiders, and other creepy-crawlies. They come in all shapes and sizes.

This is an African goliath beetle. It is the biggest and heaviest bug in the world.

The photo shows the beetle's real size.

Bug bodies

Bugs can look very different, but they have some things that are the same.

They don't have bones. Instead, they have a hard shell on the outside of their bodies.

The shell is called an exoskeleton.

This rhinoceros beetle has a very strong exoskeleton.

Bugs have at least six legs.

Some, such as millipedes, have many many more.

Bugs' bodies are made of segments joined together. Wasps have three main parts.

Thorax

Head

Abdomen

Flies have sticky feet so they can walk upside down.

Baby bugs

Most baby bugs hatch from eggs.

A mother spider lays lots of eggs. Inside each one is a baby spider.

She makes silk and wraps it around all the eggs to make an egg sac.

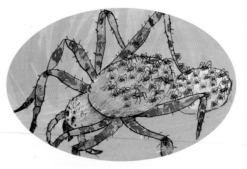

She attaches the egg sac to her body and carries it around with her.

The baby spiders grow bigger inside the eggs. Then they hatch out.

These baby shield bugs are called nymphs. Their mother is protecting them from a hungry spider.

A mother cockroach can have as many as two million babies a year!

Bug attack!

Some bugs eat other bugs
and animals for food.
They have special ways
of attacking their prey.

Scorpions use their
powerful claws
and stinging tail
to catch their prey.

In South America, giant centipedes like to eat small bats who live in dark caves.

The centipede hangs down from the cave roof. It uses its back legs to hold on.

It grabs a flying bat, injects it with poison and then eats it.

Praying mantids can turn their heads all the way around to spot their prey.

Laying a trap

Some bugs set traps to catch their prey.

An antlion digs a pit in the sand and buries itself at the bottom.

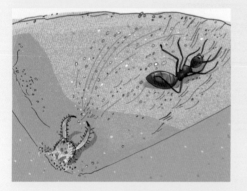

An ant falls into the pit. The antlion flicks sand at it.

The ant cannot escape. The antlion grabs it and eats it.

This spider has
made a web
out of silk.

Small bugs
fly into the
web and get
stuck. The spider
catches them
and eats them.

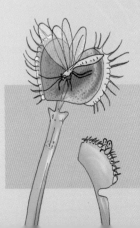

Bugs have to look out for other
traps too - a venus flytrap can
snap shut and catch them.

Stay away!

Bugs do different things to defend themselves from attack.

A swarm of hungry ants attack a bombardier beetle.

It fires boiling hot chemicals at the ants to scare them away.

This is a vinegaroon. It sprays a mist that stings its attackers.

Some caterpillars
have bright
markings and
patterns on them.

These warn other
creatures that it
is poisonous.

Stink bugs
make a nasty
smell to defend
themselves.

13

In disguise

Some bugs' bodies look like other things, which helps them hide from attackers. This is called camouflage.

Thorn bugs have spiky bodies.

They look like thorns on a stem.

This hawk moth's wings have the same pattern as the bark on a tree.

Some flies look like wasps, though they can't sting.

There's a giant leaf insect here, but it's hard to spot.

15

Wet and dry

Bugs can survive in lots of different places. They can be found in dry deserts, high up in mountains and even in icy Antarctica.

These desert grasshoppers stay buried in the sand most of the time.

When it rains, green plants grow and the grasshoppers come out to feed.

Pond skaters are very light and have legs that stretch out from their bodies.

This helps them to balance on top of the water.

A great diving beetle swims through the water.

It sees a small fish...

... and dives down quickly to catch it.

Building bugs

Some bugs work together to build a nest.

These wasps are building a paper nest. They chew wood to make a mushy pulp and build with it.

Weaver ants build their nests from leaves.

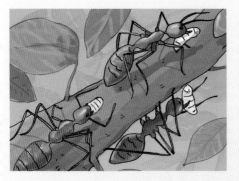

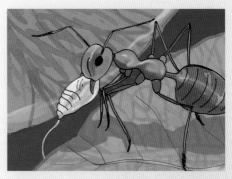

Adult ants carry young ants, called larvae, to some fresh leaves.

They gently squeeze the larvae and lots of sticky silk comes out of them.

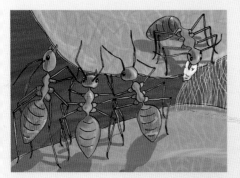

The ants use the silk to glue two leaves together. They keep adding more leaves.

They arrange the leaves into a nest and live inside it with the larvae.

High fliers

Flying bugs have thin wings that they flap very quickly to stay up in the air.

A dragonfly lays eggs underwater and nymphs hatch out of them.

A nymph lives underwater until it is fully grown. Then, it climbs up a plant.

When it is out of the water it sheds its skin. Underneath, its body and wings are soft.

The dragonfly waits until its body hardens and its wings dry out, then it flies away.

This is a May bug. It has raised its hard wing cases to free its wings.

Wing case

Its wings move so fast that they make a loud buzzing noise.

Light confuses moths, so they always fly closer to it.

Changing bugs

Many bugs change the way they look as they grow up.

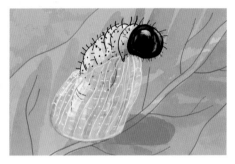

A baby caterpillar hatches out of a tiny egg and starts to eat lots of leaves.

When the caterpillar is fully grown, it hangs upside down from a branch.

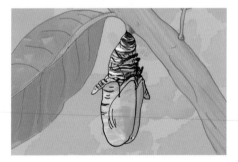

It changes into a pupa inside its skin. The old skin splits open and falls off.

Its new skin becomes a hard case. Inside, the caterpillar's body changes shape.

Two weeks later, the hard case breaks open and a butterfly with bright wings crawls out.

A butterfly's mouth is like a straw. It sucks up a sweet juice called nectar from flowers.

Bad bugs

There are some bugs in the world that are harmful to people.

Millions of desert locusts fly around together in a massive swarm.

They eat a farmer's crops until there is no food left for the farmer to eat or sell.

Killer bees often chase and sting anything that gets too close to their hive.

Flies spread germs onto food and make people sick.

Black widow spiders have a dangerous bite that kills people.

Some female mosquitoes drink blood through their straw-like mouth. This can give people a serious illness called malaria.

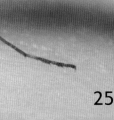

Love bugs

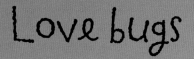

Bugs need to find a mate so they can lay eggs or have babies.

A firefly's body makes a light. It flashes it on and off to attract a mate.

Female moths make a smell that attracts lots of male moths to them.

Sometimes female bugs eat their mate.

Cicadas spend most of their lives underground, and only come above ground to find a mate.

These male cicadas make whistling, clicking or buzzing noises to attract females.

Handy helpers

Bugs do some very important jobs.

This dung beetle is rolling animal dung along the ground.

Some dung beetles bury the dung. This is good for the soil and helps plants to grow.

Bees also help plants to grow.

A bee lands on a
flower. Sticky pollen
gets stuck to the
hairs on its body.

The bee flies to
another flower.
Some of the pollen
brushes off the bee.

The flower uses the pollen
to make seeds. The seeds
turn into new plants.

Glossary of bug words

Here are some of the words in this book you might not know. This page tells you what they mean.

 exoskeleton - a hard shell on the outside of a bug's body.

 egg sac - a silky material that holds eggs inside it.

 prey - creatures that are hunted or trapped by other bugs for food.

 camouflage - a disguise that makes a bug blend in with its surroundings.

 larvae - baby bugs. Their bodies change a lot as they grow up.

 wing cases - hard cases that protect a bug's wings. Bugs raise them to fly.

 pupa - the stage between a caterpillar and an adult butterfly.

Websites to visit

You can visit exciting websites to find out more about bugs.

To visit these websites, go to the Usborne Quicklinks Website at **www.usborne-quicklinks.com** Read the internet safety guidelines, and then type the keywords "**beginners bugs**".

The websites are regularly reviewed and the links in Usborne Quicklinks are updated. However, Usborne Publishing is not responsible, and does not accept liability, for the content or availability of any website other than its own. We recommend that children are supervised while on the internet.

Many bugs hunt in flowers for food to eat.

Index

Acknowledgements

Photographic manipulation by John Russell.

Photo credits

The publishers are grateful to the following for permission to reproduce material:
© **Alamy** 20-21 (blickwinkel); © **Ardea** 25 (Steve Hopkin); © **Corbis** 4, (Wolfgang Kaehler), 11 (Oswald Eckstein/zefa), 14 (George McCarthy), 16 (Frans Lemmens/zefa); © **Digital Vision** 8; © **FLPA** Cover (Jef Meul/Foto Natura), 17 (H. Eisenbeiss), 28 (Mitsuhiko Imamori/Minden Pictures); © **Nature Picture Library** 1, 7, 18, (Kim Taylor), 2-3 (Bruce Davidson), 13 (Delpho/ARCO); © **NHPA** 12 (James Carmichael Jr), 23 (T. Kitchin & V. Hurst); © **Photolibrary.com** 14 (Brian P. Kenney); © **Science Photo Library** 15 (Richard R. Hansen), 27 (Gary Meszaros); © **Still Pictures** 5 (W. Layer); © **Superstock** 31 (age fotostock).

Every effort has been made to trace and acknowledge ownership of copyright. If any rights have been omitted, the publishers offer to rectify this in any subsequent editions following notification.